AF679655

The Path of Light: A Journey Through Sunni Mysticism

MAA

Published by MAA, 2025.

THE PATH OF LIGHT: A JOURNEY THROUGH SUNNI MYSTICISM

First edition. April 15, 2025.

ISBN: 979-8231809745

Written by MAA.

Chapter 1: Introduction to Sunni Mysticism

Sunni mysticism, also known as Tasawwuf, represents the spiritual dimension of Islam, emphasizing purification of the soul, nearness to Allah, and the pursuit of divine love. It is not a separate sect but an integral part of the Sunni Islamic tradition, rooted in the teachings of the Qur'an and the Sunnah of the Prophet Muhammad (PBUH).

The Essence of Sunni Mysticism

At its core, Sunni mysticism seeks to cultivate Ihsan—a state of excellence in worship described in the hadith of Jibril: "Ihsan is to worship Allah as if you see Him, and if you do not see Him, know that He sees you." This heightened spiritual awareness is what defines the mystical path.

Sunni mysticism is characterized by a balanced approach to spirituality, one that adheres strictly to Islamic law (Shariah) while nurturing an inner state of devotion (Haqiqah). Unlike some esoteric traditions that focus exclusively on spiritual experiences, Sunni mysticism maintains a deep connection to orthodox Islamic beliefs and practices.

The Roots of Mysticism in the Qur'an and Sunnah

The Qur'an frequently calls upon believers to engage in reflection (Tafakkur), remembrance (Dhikr), and purification of the heart (Tazkiyah). Allah says in the Qur'an:"He has succeeded who purifies it (the soul), and he has failed who instills it with corruption." (Qur'an 91:9-10).

The Prophet Muhammad (PBUH) was the ultimate example of spiritual excellence, embodying humility, patience, and love for Allah. His nights spent in deep prayer, his tears in supplication, and his unwavering trust in Allah serve as the foundation for Sunni mysticism.

Key Principles of Sunni Mysticism

Tazkiyah (Purification of the Soul): The process of cleansing one's heart from arrogance, greed, envy, and other spiritual diseases.

Dhikr (Remembrance of Allah): Regular recitation of divine names and supplications to maintain a constant awareness of Allah.

Suhbah (Spiritual Companionship): Seeking the company of righteous and pious individuals to strengthen faith.

Tawakkul (Reliance on Allah): Placing complete trust in Allah's wisdom and decree.

Mahabbah (Love of Allah and His Messenger): Cultivating a deep and sincere love for Allah and following the example of the Prophet Muhammad (PBUH).

Early Ascetics and the Development of Tasawwuf

The earliest expressions of Islamic mysticism were found among the Prophet's companions and their successors (Tabi'un), who lived simple, ascetic lives dedicated to worship and service to others. Figures such as Abu Dharr al-Ghifari and Hasan al-Basri embodied the ideals of detachment from worldly distractions and complete devotion to Allah.

As Islamic civilization expanded, spiritual masters began systematizing these principles into structured paths known as Tariqas (Sufi orders). These orders, while differing in methodology, shared a common goal: attaining closeness to Allah through disciplined practice and ethical refinement.

The Role of Sunni Mysticism in Islamic Thought

Sunni mysticism has played a vital role in shaping Islamic scholarship, culture, and ethics. Great scholars like Imam Abu Hamid Al-Ghazali worked to harmonize Tasawwuf with Islamic jurisprudence, ensuring its legitimacy within Sunni orthodoxy. He famously stated in Ihya Ulum al-Din (Revival of the Religious Sciences) that true knowledge is incomplete without spiritual realization.

Throughout history, Sunni mystics have been responsible for spreading Islam across vast regions, particularly in places like Africa, the Indian subcontinent, and Southeast Asia. Their emphasis on love, service, and humility made Islam appealing to diverse cultures.

Chapter 2: The Roots of Islamic Spirituality

The spiritual tradition in Islam is deeply rooted in the Qur'an and the Sunnah, forming the foundation upon which Islamic mysticism, or Tasawwuf, was built. Islamic spirituality is not separate from Islamic law but is, instead, its essence—guiding believers toward sincerity, purification, and a deeper connection with Allah.

The Concept of Tazkiyah (Purification of the Soul)

One of the most fundamental aspects of Islamic spirituality is Tazkiyah an-Nafs—the purification of the soul. Allah says in the Qur'an:"Indeed, he has succeeded who purifies himself." (Qur'an 87:14)This purification process involves removing negative traits such as arrogance, envy, greed, and hypocrisy, and replacing them with virtues like humility, patience, gratitude, and sincerity.

The Prophet Muhammad (PBUH) emphasized the importance of this inner purification, stating:"Verily, in the body there is a piece of flesh which, if it is sound, the entire body is sound, and if it is corrupt, the entire body is corrupt. Indeed, it is the heart." (Bukhari & Muslim)

The Role of Qur'anic Guidance in Spiritual Growth

The Qur'an repeatedly calls upon believers to engage in introspection and spiritual refinement. Among its key spiritual principles are:

Tawheed (Oneness of God): The realization that all existence depends on Allah, and only through Him can one find peace.

Tawakkul (Reliance on Allah): Trusting in Allah's wisdom and decree, even in times of hardship.

Sabr (Patience): Enduring trials with steadfastness and faith.

Shukr (Gratitude): Recognizing Allah's blessings and responding with thankfulness.

Tawbah (Repentance): Seeking Allah's forgiveness and continually striving to improve oneself.

The Sunnah as a Model for Spirituality

The life of the Prophet Muhammad (PBUH) serves as the ultimate example of Islamic spirituality. He demonstrated devotion in prayer, patience in adversity, and boundless compassion for others. His nights were spent in supplication, and his days in service to the people. His entire life was an embodiment of worship (Ibadah), sincerity (Ikhlas), and love for Allah.

Many companions of the Prophet (PBUH) followed his example by adopting ascetic practices. Figures like Abu Dharr al-Ghifari, who lived with extreme simplicity, and Salman al-Farsi, who sought spiritual wisdom from various traditions before embracing Islam, exemplified the early spirit of Tasawwuf.

The Influence of Early Muslim Scholars

Early Islamic scholars emphasized the importance of spirituality in their teachings. Hasan al-Basri, a notable early scholar, frequently warned against excessive attachment to the material world, stating: "The life of this world is nothing but an illusion. True life is found in the remembrance of Allah."

Similarly, Imam Al-Ghazali, one of the greatest Sunni scholars, stressed the necessity of balancing outward religious obligations with inner sincerity. His magnum opus, Ihya Ulum al-Din (The Revival of the Religious Sciences), systematically integrated Islamic jurisprudence with spiritual purification, making Tasawwuf accessible to mainstream Sunni thought.

The Evolution of Islamic Spirituality

As Islam spread across diverse regions, spiritual teachers established centers of learning dedicated to personal transformation. The term Sufism gradually emerged to describe these teachings, which emphasized renouncing excessive materialism and cultivating an intimate relationship with Allah through remembrance (Dhikr), reflection (Muraqabah), and love (Mahabbah).

The structured spiritual paths known as Tariqas developed as methods to preserve and transmit these teachings. These orders sought to guide students through various levels of purification, ultimately leading them toward divine proximity (Qurb).

Sunni mysticism, firmly rooted in Islamic principles, continued to flourish as an integral part of Muslim intellectual and spiritual life. From the deserts of Arabia to the mountains of Central Asia, the message of inner purification and divine love spread far and wide, shaping the spiritual landscape of the Muslim world.

Chapter 3: Understanding Tasawwuf (Sufism) in Sunni Islam

Tasawwuf, or Sufism, is often regarded as the spiritual dimension of Islam. It is the pursuit of inner purification, self-discipline, and divine love, all of which lead to a closer relationship with Allah. While some misunderstand it as a sect, Tasawwuf is deeply rooted in mainstream Sunni thought, drawing from the Qur'an, Hadith, and the practices of the Prophet Muhammad (PBUH) and his companions.

The Definition and Meaning of Tasawwuf

The term Tasawwuf is derived from the Arabic root word safa, meaning purity. This signifies that a Sufi seeks to purify their heart from worldly distractions and negative traits in order to attain spiritual closeness to Allah. Some scholars trace the term to Ahl as-Suffa, a group of ascetic companions of the Prophet (PBUH) who dedicated themselves to worship and knowledge.

In Sunni Islam, Tasawwuf is not a deviation from Shariah but a means of deepening one's adherence to it. The famous Sufi scholar Junayd al-Baghdadi described Tasawwuf as:"Tasawwuf is to act truthfully with Allah."

The Connection Between Tasawwuf and Shariah

One of the most significant misconceptions about Tasawwuf is that it contradicts Islamic law (Shariah). However, Sunni Sufis firmly uphold that Tasawwuf and Shariah are inseparable. A true Sufi is one who strictly adheres to the commands of Allah and the teachings of the Prophet Muhammad (PBUH), using the principles of Tasawwuf to enhance their faith and sincerity.

Imam Malik famously said:"He who practices Sufism without learning Sacred Law corrupts his faith, while he who learns Sacred Law without practicing Sufism corrupts himself. Only he who combines the two proves true."

The Goals of the Sufi Path

Sufism aims to cultivate several spiritual qualities in an individual:

Tazkiyah (Purification of the Soul): Refining one's character and purging spiritual diseases such as arrogance, greed, and envy.

Ihsan (Spiritual Excellence): Worshiping Allah as if one sees Him, as described in the famous Hadith of Jibreel.

Mahabbah (Divine Love): Developing an intense love for Allah and seeking His pleasure above all else.

Ma'rifah (Gnosis): Gaining deeper knowledge of Allah through personal experience and reflection.

Tawakkul (Reliance on Allah): Trusting completely in Allah's wisdom and decree.

The Practices of Tasawwuf

To achieve these goals, Sufis engage in various practices, including:

Dhikr (Remembrance of Allah): Repeating the names of Allah or specific supplications to cleanse the heart.

Muraqabah (Spiritual Reflection): Meditating on one's actions and intentions to maintain sincerity.

Khalwa (Seclusion): Withdrawing temporarily from distractions to focus on worship.

Sohbet (Spiritual Companionship): Keeping the company of righteous individuals to strengthen one's faith.

The Role of a Shaykh (Spiritual Guide)

In Tasawwuf, a Murshid (spiritual guide) plays a crucial role in helping seekers navigate the spiritual path. This relationship is based on trust, knowledge, and wisdom, ensuring that the student does not fall into extremes or self-delusion.

Sunni Sufi orders, such as the Naqshbandi, Qadiri, Chishti, and Shadhili orders, have historically preserved this tradition by providing structured guidance for seekers. These teachers emphasize a balanced approach, ensuring that their students uphold Islamic teachings while cultivating inner spirituality.

The Misconceptions Surrounding Sufism

Many critics of Sufism misunderstand its principles due to the actions of misguided individuals who claim to be Sufis but deviate from Islamic teachings. Authentic Tasawwuf always upholds the Qur'an and Sunnah, rejecting innovations (bid'ah) that contradict Islamic law. Prominent scholars such as Imam Al-Ghazali, Ibn Taymiyyah, and Shah Waliullah acknowledged the value of genuine Tasawwuf when practiced correctly.

Sufism is not about superstitions or exaggerated rituals but about purifying the heart and deepening one's connection with Allah. It has played a vital role in spreading Islam, fostering love, tolerance, and devotion among Muslims throughout history.

Chapter 4: The Qur'an and Hadith: Foundations of Mystical Thought

The Qur'an and Hadith form the primary sources of Islamic knowledge and guidance, including the mystical dimensions of faith. Sunni mysticism, or Tasawwuf, finds its legitimacy and inspiration deeply embedded in these sacred texts. Sufis interpret these sources not only for legal and theological insights but also for their spiritual and esoteric meanings.

The Qur'an as the Source of Mystical Insight

The Qur'an repeatedly emphasizes introspection, remembrance of Allah (dhikr), and the purification of the soul (tazkiyah), all of which are central to Sufi thought. Verses such as:

"Indeed, he succeeds who purifies himself." (Qur'an 87:14)

"Verily, in the remembrance of Allah do hearts find rest." (Qur'an 13:28)

These verses encourage a deep spiritual connection with the Divine, beyond mere ritualistic worship. Sunni mystics believe that understanding the Qur'an requires not only intellectual study but also inner realization, which is nurtured through practices like contemplation (tafakkur) and spiritual exercises.

The Role of Hadith in Sufi Teachings

The sayings of the Prophet Muhammad (PBUH) provide further clarity on spiritual excellence (ihsan) and inner purification. A foundational hadith describing ihsan states:

"Ihsan is to worship Allah as if you see Him, for if you do not see Him, He surely sees you." (Sahih Muslim)

This hadith encapsulates the Sufi aspiration of attaining closeness to Allah through deep awareness and sincerity. The Prophet (PBUH) himself exemplified asceticism (zuhd), humility, and unwavering devotion, serving as the ultimate model for those seeking a mystical connection with the Divine.

Qur'anic Themes in Sunni Mysticism

Sunni mystics derive core principles from the Qur'an, including:

Tawhid (Oneness of God): The fundamental belief in Allah's absolute unity and transcendence, which forms the basis for spiritual devotion.

Tazkiyah (Purification): The Qur'an stresses the need for cleansing the heart of arrogance, greed, and heedlessness.

Dhikr (Remembrance of Allah): Many verses highlight the importance of constantly remembering Allah.

Sabr (Patience) and **Shukr** (Gratitude): Essential qualities for spiritual seekers striving for closeness to Allah.

Divine Love: The Qur'an mentions Allah's love for His servants and their reciprocal love for Him.

Hadiths on the Inner Dimensions of Faith

Beyond legal injunctions, numerous hadiths emphasize sincerity, humility, and reliance on Allah (tawakkul). For example:

"Allah does not look at your bodies nor your forms, but He looks at your hearts and your deeds." (Sahih Muslim)

This hadith underscores the significance of inner purification over mere outward conformity to rituals, a theme central to Sunni mysticism.

The Prophet Muhammad (PBUH)

The life of the Prophet (PBUH) serves as a blueprint for spiritual seekers. His deep contemplation in the cave of Hira, his night prayers (tahajjud), and his profound humility demonstrate the essence of a mystical path grounded in divine love and devotion.

Sunni mystics regard him as the perfect model of spirituality, embodying the balance between outward religious practice (Shariah) and inward spiritual realization (Haqiqah). His interactions with the Ahl as-Suffa, a group of devoted ascetics who lived in simplicity near the Prophet's mosque, further highlight the roots of Islamic mysticism.

Chapter 5: The Role of the Prophet Muhammad (PBUH) in Mysticism

The Prophet Muhammad (PBUH) holds a central place in Sunni mysticism as the perfect embodiment of both the outer and inner dimensions of Islam. His life provides an ideal model for those seeking a deeper connection with Allah, blending obedience to divine law (Shariah) with inner spiritual realization (Haqiqah). Sunni mystics view him as the ultimate spiritual guide, whose teachings and practices illuminate the path of Tasawwuf.

The Prophet (PBUH) as the Seal of Mystical Guidance

Sufis regard the Prophet Muhammad (PBUH) as the Insan al-Kamil (the Perfect Man), the highest example of spiritual excellence. His life was not only one of religious instruction but also one of profound spiritual depth. His seclusion in the Cave of Hira, his nightly devotions (tahajjud), and his intimate supplications to Allah reveal a deeply mystical aspect of his character.

The Qur'an confirms his role as a guide for those seeking purification:

"It is He who has sent among the unlettered a Messenger from themselves, reciting to them His verses, purifying them and teaching them the Book and wisdom." (Qur'an 62:2)

This verse establishes the Prophet's role in spiritual purification (tazkiyah), a central concept in Sunni mysticism.

The Prophet's Ascension (Isra and Miraj) as a Mystical Experience

One of the most profound spiritual events in the life of the Prophet (PBUH) was the Isra and Miraj—his night journey and ascension to the heavens. This event is often interpreted by Sunni mystics as an example of spiritual elevation, symbolizing the seeker's journey toward divine closeness. The ascension represents the possibility of transcending worldly attachments and attaining ma'rifah (direct knowledge of Allah).

Mystics believe that just as the Prophet (PBUH) traveled beyond the physical realms to witness divine realities, sincere seekers can also ascend spiritually through devotion, remembrance (dhikr), and purification of the heart.

The Prophet's Connection to the Sufi Orders

All Sunni Sufi orders trace their spiritual lineage (silsilah) back to the Prophet Muhammad (PBUH). This chain of transmission is crucial in ensuring the authenticity and continuity of mystical teachings. The Prophet's close companions, particularly Abu Bakr As-Siddiq (RA) and Ali ibn Abi Talib (RA), are seen as key transmitters of the esoteric dimensions of Islam.

The Naqshbandi order, for example, claims a direct link to Abu Bakr (RA), while the Qadiri, Chishti, and Shadhili orders trace their lineage through Ali (RA). These companions played a significant role in preserving the Prophet's spiritual wisdom and passing it down through generations of scholars and mystics.

The Prophet's Practices That Influenced Sunni Mysticism

Many of the Prophet's personal practices form the foundation of Sufi rituals and disciplines. Some of the most significant include:

Dhikr (Remembrance of Allah): The Prophet (PBUH) encouraged his companions to engage in constant remembrance of Allah, a practice central to all Sufi orders.

"Shall I not inform you of the best of your deeds, the purest in the sight of your Lord, and the highest in reward? It is the remembrance of Allah." (Sunan Ibn Majah)

Tafakkur (Contemplation): The Prophet spent long periods in contemplation, particularly in the Cave of Hira before receiving revelation. Sufis emphasize meditation and self-reflection as a means of spiritual insight.

Tahajjud (Night Prayer): The Prophet's devotion to night prayers exemplified the discipline of voluntary worship, which many Sufis adopt as a means of spiritual purification.

Zuhd (Asceticism): The Prophet lived a simple life, detaching himself from worldly excess. His minimalism and focus on the hereafter deeply influence Sufi ideals of renunciation and reliance on Allah (tawakkul).

Ihsan (Spiritual Excellence): As defined in the famous hadith of Jibreel, ihsan is the highest level of faith. The Prophet's life is the ultimate example of this inward excellence, which Sufis strive to achieve.

The Prophet's Love and Mercy as the Essence of Mysticism

Sufis emphasize the deep love the Prophet (PBUH) had for humanity, as seen in the Qur'an:

"And We have not sent you, [O Muhammad], except as a mercy to the worlds." (Qur'an 21:107)

This boundless compassion is considered a fundamental trait of the mystic. Love (mahabbah) and mercy (rahmah) are central themes in Sunni Sufi teachings, with the Prophet serving as the ultimate manifestation of these qualities. His love for Allah and for creation sets the standard for the wayfarer (salik) on the mystical path.

Chapter 6: The Concept of Ihsan: Spiritual Excellence

Ihsan, the highest level of spiritual realization in Islam, plays a crucial role in Sunni mysticism. Rooted in the famous hadith of Jibreel, Ihsan is defined as "to worship Allah as though you see Him, and if you cannot see Him, then indeed He sees you." This concept bridges outward religious observance with inner spiritual consciousness, shaping the mystical path.

Ihsan in the Qur'an and Hadith

The Qur'an frequently emphasizes the virtue of Ihsan:

"Indeed, Allah is with those who practice Ihsan." (Qur'an 16:128)

This divine companionship reflects the deep connection between the seeker and the Divine, where sincerity and excellence in worship bring one closer to Allah. The Prophet Muhammad (PBUH) also stressed the importance of Ihsan in daily life, extending it beyond prayer to acts of kindness, honesty, and humility.

Ihsan as the Inner Dimension of Faith

Sunni mysticism views Ihsan as the soul of religious practice. While Islam encompasses outward rituals (Shariah) and Iman represents belief, Ihsan embodies the inner transformation that aligns the heart with divine reality. This spiritual excellence is not limited to worship but permeates every aspect of a believer's life, cultivating sincerity (ikhlas), gratitude (shukr), and patience (sabr).

The Role of Ihsan in Purification of the Heart

A fundamental aspect of Sunni mysticism is tazkiyah—the purification of the heart. Ihsan serves as the guiding principle in this process, requiring the seeker to develop awareness of Allah (muraqaba) and constantly refine their intentions. This purification involves:

Cleansing the heart of arrogance, envy, and heedlessness

Developing qualities like humility, sincerity, and compassion

Strengthening one's connection to Allah through remembrance (dhikr)

Ihsan and Spiritual Awakening

Ihsan leads the mystic to higher states of spiritual consciousness. Through sincerity in worship and mindfulness of Allah's presence, the seeker moves from ritualistic practice to intimate divine awareness. This heightened state of perception is often described as ma'rifah (gnosis), where knowledge of Allah transcends intellectual understanding and becomes an experiential reality.

The Continuous Struggle for Ihsan

Achieving Ihsan is an ongoing journey rather than a fixed state. Sunni mystics emphasize the necessity of perseverance, self-discipline, and reliance on Allah (tawakkul). The struggle against the lower self (nafs) remains a central challenge, requiring constant effort and divine assistance.

Chapter 7: Major Sunni Sufi Orders: Naqshbandi, Qadiri, Chishti, and Shadhili

Sunni mysticism has given rise to various Sufi orders, each embodying unique spiritual methodologies while remaining rooted in the fundamental principles of Tasawwuf. Among these, the Naqshbandi, Qadiri, Chishti, and Shadhili orders are the most prominent, each contributing distinct practices and teachings to the mystical tradition.

The Naqshbandi Order: Silent Dhikr and Inner Awareness

The Naqshbandi order, founded by Baha-ud-Din Naqshband (d. 1389), emphasizes silent remembrance (dhikr khafi) and inner contemplation. Unlike other Sufi paths that encourage vocal chanting, the Naqshbandis focus on internalizing divine remembrance within the heart. Their method is often described as "the silent path," where spiritual progress is attained through deep self-discipline, mindfulness of Allah, and strict adherence to the Sunnah.

The Qadiri Order: The Path of Divine Grace

Founded by Abdul Qadir Jilani (d. 1166), the Qadiri order is known for its emphasis on divine grace (barakah) and strong reliance on the remembrance of Allah (dhikr). Qadiri teachings stress generosity, humility, and service to humanity. Their spiritual practices include both individual and collective dhikr, often expressed through rhythmic chanting and supplications. The Qadiri path encourages an open-hearted connection to the Divine and deep trust in Allah's mercy.

The Chishti Order: Love and Devotion

The Chishti order, established by Khwaja Moinuddin Chishti (d. 1236) in the Indian subcontinent, is renowned for its emphasis on love, tolerance, and service to others. The Chishti path prioritizes sama (spiritual music and poetry) as a means of reaching divine ecstasy. This order places great importance on the concept of ishq (divine love), encouraging seekers to express their devotion through acts of kindness and selflessness. The Chishti Sufis have historically played a significant role in fostering interfaith harmony and promoting inclusivity.

The Shadhili Order: Practical Spirituality

Founded by Abu'l-Hasan al-Shadhili (d. 1258), the Shadhili order integrates spirituality into daily life, encouraging disciples to remain engaged in worldly affairs while maintaining a deep connection to Allah. Unlike other Sufi paths that emphasize asceticism, the Shadhili approach teaches that one can attain closeness to Allah while actively participating in society. Their teachings stress reliance on Allah (tawakkul), remembrance through wird (regular litanies), and spiritual insight (ma'rifah).

The Unity of Sufi Orders

While each order follows distinct practices, they all share a common goal: spiritual purification and closeness to Allah. The differences in approach reflect the diverse needs of seekers, ensuring that individuals from varying backgrounds and temperaments can find a path suited to their spiritual journey. Ultimately, the Sufi orders function as interconnected rivers leading to the same ocean of divine love and enlightenment.

Chapter 8: The Role of a Murshid (Spiritual Guide)

The presence of a Murshid (spiritual guide) is essential in the path of Sunni mysticism. The Murshid, also known as a Shaykh or Pir, serves as a mentor who provides wisdom, direction, and personal support to the seeker (murid). Their role extends beyond teaching; they nurture the spiritual development of their disciples and help them navigate the challenges of the mystical journey.

The Qualifications of a Murshid

A Murshid must embody deep piety, knowledge, and an unshakable connection to Allah. They are expected to adhere strictly to the teachings of the Qur'an and Sunnah while possessing an understanding of Tasawwuf's inner dimensions. A true guide does not seek worldly gain but rather dedicates their life to helping others reach spiritual enlightenment.

The Relationship Between Murshid and Murid

The connection between a Murshid and a Murid is built on trust, sincerity, and obedience. The Murid commits to learning under the guidance of their Murshid, following their instructions with humility and dedication. In return, the Murshid provides spiritual prescriptions, advises on personal struggles, and offers prayers for the Murid's progress. This relationship is based on love and mutual respect, forming the foundation for transformation.

The Role of the Murshid in Spiritual Training

A Murshid leads disciples through stages of purification, focusing on three core aspects:

Tazkiyah (Purification of the Soul) – Removing negative traits such as arrogance, envy, and greed.

Tarbiya (Spiritual Nurturing) – Strengthening faith through disciplined worship and devotion.

Irfan (Spiritual Insight) – Cultivating deep understanding and awareness of the Divine.

Methods of Guidance

Murshids use various approaches to help their students advance spiritually:

Dhikr (Remembrance of Allah): Assigning specific litanies or supplications to increase spiritual awareness.

Muraqaba (Meditation): Teaching contemplation techniques to attain higher consciousness of Allah.

Adab (Spiritual Etiquette): Instructing in moral refinement and behavior that aligns with Islamic teachings.

Suhbah (Company of the Righteous): Encouraging association with pious individuals to strengthen faith.

The Ethical Conduct of a Murshid

A Murshid must uphold the highest ethical standards, leading by example. They must remain humble, truthful, and dedicated to serving Allah and His creation. Any form of spiritual abuse or exploitation is a violation of trust and disqualifies one from true guidance.

The Murshid's Impact on the Seeker

With the right guidance, a Murid develops sincerity, discipline, and an unwavering connection to Allah. The Murshid helps the seeker move beyond superficial religiosity, allowing them to experience the depth of faith. Through patience and perseverance, the Murid gradually attains spiritual closeness to the Divine.

Chapter 9: The Path of the Seeker (Salik)

The journey of the seeker (Salik) in Sunni mysticism is one of discipline, sincerity, and spiritual refinement. It is a path that demands unwavering commitment to Allah, self-purification, and the continuous struggle against the lower self (nafs). The Salik undertakes a transformative process that deepens their awareness of the Divine and brings them closer to ultimate truth.

The Stages of the Seeker's Path

The journey of the Salik unfolds in distinct stages, each marking a deeper level of spiritual awareness:

Tawba (Repentance): The first step in the path is sincere repentance, turning away from sin and seeking Allah's forgiveness with the intention of living a life of righteousness.

Mujahada (Spiritual Struggle): The seeker must engage in an internal battle against the desires of the ego, ensuring their actions align with divine guidance.

Tazkiyah (Purification of the Heart): Removing arrogance, envy, and heedlessness, replacing them with humility, gratitude, and mindfulness of Allah.

Tawakkul (Trust in Allah): Developing complete reliance on Allah's wisdom, surrendering personal concerns and attachments.

Mahabba (Divine Love): Cultivating love for Allah and His Messenger (PBUH), allowing that love to shape one's character and actions.

Ma'rifah (Gnosis): Gaining deep insight into the nature of existence, the self, and the reality of Divine presence.

The Role of Discipline and Devotion

The Salik's progress depends on disciplined adherence to spiritual practices. This includes:

Regular Dhikr (Remembrance of Allah): Reciting specific litanies to keep the heart focused on the Divine.

Salah (Prayer) with Presence: Performing prayers with sincerity and mindfulness, seeing them as moments of connection rather than routine obligations.

Fasting and Self-Restraint: Using fasting as a means of controlling desires and refining spiritual perception.

Seeking Knowledge: Studying the Qur'an, Hadith, and the teachings of great mystics to cultivate wisdom and spiritual depth.

Overcoming Spiritual Obstacles

The path is not without its challenges. The Salik may experience doubt, distractions, and moments of despair. However, perseverance, reliance on Allah, and guidance from a Murshid help the seeker remain steadfast. The purification of the heart is a gradual process, requiring patience and sincerity.

The Fruits of the Journey

As the Salik advances, they attain increasing levels of inner peace, divine proximity, and moral refinement. Their perception of reality becomes clearer, seeing Allah's signs in all things. The journey leads to deep tranquility, spiritual wisdom, and a love that transcends worldly concerns.

Chapter 10: The Importance of Dhikr (Remembrance of Allah)

Dhikr, the remembrance of Allah, is one of the most central and transformative practices in Sunni mysticism. It is the means by which the heart is purified, the soul is drawn closer to Allah, and the individual achieves spiritual elevation. Dhikr is not only an act of worship but also a state of being, in which the seeker remains constantly aware of the Divine presence.

The Spiritual Significance of Dhikr

Dhikr is mentioned repeatedly in the Qur'an as a path to attaining tranquility and divine proximity. Allah states:

"Verily, in the remembrance of Allah do hearts find rest." (Qur'an 13:28)

It is through Dhikr that the soul is freed from distractions and worldly burdens, allowing the seeker to focus entirely on their Creator. The practice strengthens faith, fosters sincerity, and instills deep contentment in the heart.

Forms of Dhikr

Dhikr takes many forms, each serving a unique purpose in spiritual development. Some of the most common forms include:

Tasbih (Glorification of Allah): Reciting phrases such as SubhanAllah (Glory be to Allah), Alhamdulillah (All praise is due to Allah), and Allahu Akbar (Allah is the Greatest) to maintain a consciousness of divine majesty.

Tahlil (Affirmation of Divine Unity): Repeating La ilaha illa Allah (There is no god but Allah) to reaffirm one's faith in Tawhid, the oneness of God.

Salawat (Sending Blessings on the Prophet PBUH): Reciting Allahumma salli 'ala Muhammad wa 'ala aali Muhammad (O Allah, send blessings upon Muhammad and his family) as a means of seeking intercession and drawing closer to the Prophet's example.

Qur'anic Recitation: Engaging in the reading and recitation of the Qur'an with reflection and contemplation.

Silent and Vocal Dhikr: Dhikr may be performed audibly in a gathering or silently within the heart, both of which are valid and carry immense spiritual benefit.

The Role of Dhikr in Purification of the Heart

The heart is the center of spiritual perception in Islamic mysticism. A heart that is heedless of Allah becomes hardened, while one that is engaged in constant remembrance attains illumination. Dhikr serves to cleanse the heart from spiritual diseases such as arrogance, envy, and heedlessness. The Prophet Muhammad (PBUH) likened Dhikr to polishing a rusty object, restoring its luster and clarity.

The Benefits of Dhikr

Engaging in regular remembrance of Allah yields profound effects on both the inner self and daily life. Among its benefits are:

Strengthening One's Connection with Allah: The more one remembers Allah, the more they become aware of His presence in all aspects of life.

Attaining Inner Peace: Dhikr instills tranquility, allowing one to navigate life's challenges with patience and faith.

Protection from Negative Influences: The remembrance of Allah serves as a shield against evil thoughts and external temptations.

Increased Spiritual Insight: Regular Dhikr opens the heart to divine wisdom, allowing one to perceive deeper truths.

Collective and Individual Dhikr

Dhikr can be practiced individually or in gatherings (halqas). While personal remembrance fosters a private connection with Allah, collective Dhikr strengthens communal bonds and amplifies spiritual energy. Many Sunni Sufi orders conduct Dhikr circles, where seekers engage in synchronized recitations, fostering a shared experience of divine presence.

Dhikr as a Way of Life

True Dhikr extends beyond verbal recitation. It manifests in one's actions, character, and interactions. A person who embodies Dhikr walks through life with humility, gratitude, and consciousness of Allah. Ultimately, Dhikr is not only about remembering Allah at specific times but about living in a state of continuous awareness and devotion.

Chapter 11: Fana and Baqa: Annihilation and Subsistence

Fana (annihilation) and Baqa (subsistence) are two of the most profound concepts in Sunni mysticism. These stages mark the seeker's transformation as they move closer to Allah, transcending the ego and immersing themselves in divine reality. While Fana represents the dissolution of the self, Baqa signifies the establishment of a higher, enlightened existence aligned with the divine will.

The Meaning of Fana (Annihilation)

Fana is the spiritual state in which the seeker's sense of personal identity is obliterated, leaving only a profound awareness of Allah. It is not a loss of existence but rather a dissolution of the ego and its attachments. In this state, all distractions, desires, and worldly inclinations fade away, allowing the seeker to experience the pure presence of the Divine.

The Qur'an alludes to this transformation:

"Everything will perish except His face." (Qur'an 28:88)

Many Sufi masters describe Fana as a necessary stage in reaching true servitude to Allah. The seeker does not cease to exist physically but transcends personal inclinations, seeing themselves only as an instrument of divine will. It is a state where self-centeredness is replaced with full submission and reliance on Allah.

The Process of Fana

The path to Fana involves:

Detachment from Worldly Distractions: The seeker gradually loses interest in material pursuits, focusing instead on spiritual realities.

Negation of the Self: The ego, which fuels pride and self-importance, is stripped away through prayer, dhikr, and spiritual discipline.

Complete Surrender to Allah: The seeker becomes aware that everything they are and do is by Allah's will, leading to total reliance on Him.

Fana is often described as an overwhelming experience of divine nearness. The seeker's sense of individuality fades, replaced by an awareness that only Allah remains. This is not a permanent state, but a transformative passage leading to Baqa.

The Meaning of Baqa (Subsistence)

Baqa follows Fana, representing the stage where the seeker, having annihilated the ego, now exists in a state of enlightened awareness and submission to Allah. While Fana is about losing the self, Baqa is about returning to the world with a renewed perspective, living with divine consciousness in every action and thought.

Baqa is the station of prophets and saints—those who, after dissolving their lower selves, remain in perfect harmony with the will of Allah. Their existence is no longer driven by personal desires but by divine purpose.

The Effects of Baqa

A person who attains Baqa:

Lives with constant awareness of Allah in every moment.

Acts solely for the sake of Allah, not for personal gain or recognition.

Becomes a vessel of divine mercy and wisdom, radiating spiritual insight and love.

Engages with the world but remains detached from its illusions and distractions.

The Relationship Between Fana and Baqa

Fana and Baqa are two sides of the same journey. One must first annihilate the ego to reach a state where divine presence can fully manifest. Once that presence is realized, the seeker returns to the world with a transformed understanding, engaging with life not as an individual striving for personal gain, but as a servant of Allah, upholding truth, justice, and love.

These states are not exclusive to saints or mystics; they represent the ultimate goal of every sincere believer striving for closeness to Allah. Through constant remembrance, devotion, and spiritual discipline, anyone can experience a degree of Fana and Baqa in their personal journey toward divine reality.

Chapter 12: The Spiritual Stations (Maqamat) and States (Ahwal)

Sunni mysticism describes the spiritual journey as a progression through different stages of self-purification and divine proximity. These stages, known as Maqamat (stations), and Ahwal (states), map out the internal transformation of the seeker as they strive for closeness to Allah. Unlike Maqamat, which are acquired through effort and discipline, Ahwal are divine gifts granted to the seeker at Allah's discretion.

The Spiritual Stations (Maqamat)

The Maqamat are fixed stages of spiritual discipline that a seeker must pass through on their journey. Each station represents a higher level of purification and devotion. Some of the key stations include:

Tawbah (Repentance): The first step in the spiritual path, where the seeker sincerely repents for past sins and turns towards Allah with a purified heart.

Zuhd (Detachment): A state of renouncing worldly distractions and material desires to focus entirely on spiritual growth.

Sabr (Patience): The seeker learns to endure hardships and trials without losing faith, trusting that Allah's wisdom governs all things.

Shukr (Gratitude): The heart becomes grateful for both blessings and trials, recognizing that everything comes from Allah.

Tawakkul (Trust in Allah): A deep reliance on Allah, surrendering personal concerns and placing absolute trust in His plan.

Rida (Contentment): Accepting Allah's decree with a peaceful heart, no longer disturbed by the ups and downs of life.

Mahabbah (Love of Allah): A stage where the seeker's devotion turns into pure love, desiring nothing except closeness to the Divine.

Each Maqam requires conscious effort, self-discipline, and inner reflection. The seeker cannot move to a higher station without mastering the one before it.

The Spiritual States (Ahwal)

Unlike Maqamat, Ahwal are spiritual conditions that come and go without the seeker's control. They are divine gifts rather than personal achievements. Some important Ahwal include:

Wajd (Ecstasy): An overwhelming feeling of divine presence, often experienced during dhikr or deep contemplation.

Sukr (Intoxication): A mystical state where the love of Allah becomes so intense that the seeker loses awareness of anything else.

Bast (Expansion): A state of spiritual joy and lightness, where the heart feels free and at peace.

Qabd (Constriction): A temporary state of spiritual difficulty, where the seeker feels distant from Allah as a test of patience and sincerity.

Tajalli (Divine Manifestation): Moments when the seeker perceives divine truths with absolute clarity.

The Relationship Between Maqamat and Ahwal

While Maqamat are milestones that require effort and commitment, Ahwal are temporary experiences that come as blessings. A seeker may move through different Ahwal multiple times throughout their journey, whereas Maqamat represent lasting spiritual progress.

Understanding these stages helps the seeker remain steadfast, recognizing that challenges and moments of bliss are part of the divine process. By embracing both the struggles and the blessings, they draw ever closer to the reality of Allah's presence.

Chapter 13: The Role of Love in Sunni Mysticism

Love is a central force in Sunni mysticism, serving as the foundation for the seeker's journey toward Allah. It transcends worldly attachments and elevates the heart to a state of divine intimacy. In the teachings of Sunni Sufism, love is not merely an emotion but a transformative force that purifies the soul and draws it closer to the Divine.

The Love of Allah (Mahabbatullah)

The highest form of love in Sunni mysticism is the love of Allah. This love is rooted in the Qur'an, where Allah describes Himself as "Al-Wadud" (The Most Loving). The Qur'an states: "Those who believe are stronger in love for Allah" (2:165). This love compels the seeker to long for Allah's presence, to remember Him constantly, and to obey His commands out of devotion rather than fear.

Love for the Prophet Muhammad (PBUH)

A fundamental aspect of mystical love is deep reverence and devotion to the Prophet Muhammad (PBUH). Sunni mystics view him as the perfect manifestation of divine love and mercy. Loving him means following his Sunnah, embodying his character, and cultivating the virtues he taught. The Prophet himself said, "None of you truly believes until I am more beloved to him than his father, his child, and all of mankind."

Love as a Means of Spiritual Transformation

In the path of Tasawwuf, love is seen as the fire that burns away the veils of the ego and worldly attachments. The seeker who truly loves Allah and His Messenger experiences a shift in their inner world—desires become aligned with divine will, and personal ambitions give way to servitude to Allah. Love transforms the heart into a vessel of divine presence, allowing the seeker to experience the sweetness of faith (halawat al-iman).

The Role of Ishq (Intense Love) in Sufism

Sufi poetry and teachings often refer to Ishq, an intense, selfless love that consumes the seeker's being. Ishq drives the mystic beyond intellectual understanding and into experiential knowledge of the Divine. Poets such as Rumi and Hafiz have described this love as a fire that annihilates the self, leaving only the radiance of Allah's presence.

The Balance Between Love and Fear

While love is a guiding force, Sunni mysticism also teaches that it must be balanced with reverence (khashyah) and awe of Allah. The great Sufi master Junayd al-Baghdadi stated that true seekers walk the path with both "wings of love and fear." Love draws them closer, while awe ensures humility and sincerity.

Expressions of Love in Practice

Mystical love manifests through various acts of devotion:

Dhikr (Remembrance of Allah): Constant remembrance strengthens love and deepens divine connection.

Salawat (Sending Blessings on the Prophet): Repeating prayers upon the Prophet cultivates love and aligns the heart with his teachings.

Service to Others: Love is expressed through acts of kindness, generosity, and selflessness, mirroring the Prophetic example.

By cultivating love in these ways, the seeker moves ever closer to Allah, experiencing a profound inner transformation that reshapes their very existence.

Chapter 14: The Concept of Tawakkul (Trust in Allah)

Tawakkul, or trust in Allah, is a foundational principle in Sunni mysticism. It signifies a deep reliance on the Divine, recognizing that all affairs are ultimately in His control. For the seeker on the spiritual path, tawakkul is not a passive resignation to fate, but an active surrender, coupled with effort, patience, and unwavering faith.

The Qur'anic Basis of Tawakkul

The Qur'an repeatedly emphasizes the importance of trust in Allah. One of the most profound verses states: "And whoever relies upon Allah – then He is sufficient for him" (65:3). This verse encapsulates the essence of tawakkul, assuring the believer that true reliance on Allah brings divine sufficiency and guidance. Another verse instructs: "Upon Allah let the believers rely" (3:122), reinforcing that reliance is a sign of faith.

Tawakkul and the Prophetic Example

The life of the Prophet Muhammad (PBUH) provides a perfect model of tawakkul. Despite facing immense challenges, he never wavered in his trust in Allah. From the migration to Madinah to the trials of battle, he demonstrated a balanced approach—taking necessary action while placing complete trust in divine decree. His supplication, "O Allah, I surrender myself to You, and I turn my affairs over to You", highlights the essence of true reliance.

The Balance Between Effort and Reliance

Sunni mysticism teaches that tawakkul does not mean abandoning effort. Instead, it requires a balance between working diligently and surrendering the outcome to Allah. The well-known hadith illustrates this balance: A man asked the Prophet (PBUH), "Should I tie my camel and trust in Allah, or leave it untied and trust in Him?" The Prophet replied, "Tie your camel and trust in Allah." This wisdom underscores that reliance on Allah should never be an excuse for negligence or inaction.

Tawakkul as a Spiritual State

In the journey of Tasawwuf, tawakkul is more than a belief—it is a state of the heart. A seeker who attains true trust in Allah is free from anxiety and fear, knowing that whatever happens is by His divine wisdom. Imam Al-Ghazali describes tawakkul as a condition in which the heart rests in Allah's decree, unaffected by worldly uncertainties. Such a state brings peace and contentment, as the seeker no longer depends on material security but on divine sufficiency.

The Fruits of Tawakkul

A person who truly embodies tawakkul experiences several profound benefits:

Inner Tranquility: Worries and anxieties diminish when one entrusts all matters to Allah.

Strength in Trials: Hardships become bearable, as the believer sees them as part of Allah's divine plan.

Increased Gratitude: Recognizing that all provisions come from Allah cultivates deep gratitude.

Sincerity in Worship: The heart detaches from worldly reliance and focuses entirely on Allah.

Practicing Tawakkul in Daily Life

To develop tawakkul, a seeker must:

Strengthen their faith by reflecting on Allah's attributes of mercy, wisdom, and power.

Increase remembrance of Allah (dhikr) to reinforce trust in Him.

Make dua (supplication), asking Allah to instill true reliance in their heart.

Detach from excessive worry about the future, knowing that Allah's plan is always best.

Tawakkul is not merely a theological concept but a lived reality for the mystic. It transforms fear into faith, anxiety into peace, and uncertainty into unwavering trust in the Divine.

Chapter 15: The Role of Fasting and Seclusion in Spiritual Growth

Fasting and seclusion hold a profound place in Sunni mysticism, serving as means of purification, self-discipline, and spiritual elevation. These practices help the seeker detach from worldly distractions, allowing for an intensified focus on the remembrance of Allah.

Fasting: A Path to Inner Purification

Fasting, particularly beyond Ramadan, is considered a means of refining the soul. The Prophet Muhammad (PBUH) encouraged fasting on Mondays and Thursdays as well as on the White Days (13th, 14th, and 15th of each lunar month). For the Sufi seeker, fasting is not merely about abstaining from food and drink but about controlling desires, refining character, and strengthening reliance on Allah.

The Qur'an states: "O you who have believed, fasting has been prescribed for you as it was prescribed for those before you that you may attain taqwa" (2:183). Taqwa, or God-consciousness, is the essence of fasting in the mystical path—it elevates the seeker beyond physical deprivation to a heightened spiritual state.

Fasting as a Shield Against the Ego

One of the primary obstacles in the journey toward Allah is the nafs (lower self), which inclines toward heedlessness and indulgence. Fasting weakens the hold of the nafs, creating a state of humility and dependency on Allah. Many Sufi masters advocate prolonged fasting as a way to discipline the soul and cultivate patience, sincerity, and gratitude.

Seclusion (Khalwa) in Sunni Mysticism

Seclusion, or khalwa, is another powerful practice for spiritual refinement. It involves temporarily withdrawing from society to focus on dhikr, prayer, and reflection. The Prophet (PBUH) himself engaged in seclusion in the Cave of Hira before receiving revelation, setting a precedent for deep spiritual introspection.

The great Sufi masters often prescribed khalwa to their disciples to remove distractions and purify the heart. Imam Al-Ghazali, in Ihya Ulum al-Din, describes seclusion as a means of silencing worldly noise, allowing the seeker to hear the whispers of the soul and the divine call of Allah.

The Conditions of Khalwa

While seclusion is beneficial, it requires guidance. A murshid (spiritual guide) often instructs the seeker on how to properly engage in solitude without falling into excessive isolation. The key aspects of khalwa include:

A purified intention—Seclusion is for Allah alone, not for self-glorification or escapism.

Structured spiritual practices—Dhikr, recitation of the Qur'an, and reflection on one's state are central.

A balance between isolation and engagement—Seclusion should strengthen one's ability to return to society with greater spiritual insight.

The Fruits of Fasting and Seclusion

When practiced with sincerity, fasting and seclusion lead to:

Heightened awareness of Allah—Detachment from physical needs strengthens one's connection to the Divine.

Mastery over the nafs—The ego loses its grip, allowing the heart to become more receptive to divine guidance.

Spiritual illumination—Many seekers report moments of deep insight and tranquility during periods of fasting and seclusion.

Both fasting and seclusion are tools of transformation, bringing the seeker closer to Allah through discipline, patience, and introspection. They are not meant for self-denial alone but as pathways to an enriched inner life rooted in divine love and awareness.

Chapter 16: The Mystical Dimensions of Prayer (Salah)

Prayer (Salah) is the cornerstone of a Muslim's spiritual life, but within Sunni mysticism, it carries deeper significance beyond its outward form. The five daily prayers serve not only as acts of worship but also as moments of divine connection, purification, and transcendence.

Salah as a Spiritual Ascent

The Prophet Muhammad (PBUH) described prayer as the believer's ascension (mi'raj), a direct communication with Allah. Sufi masters emphasize that in true prayer, the heart must be present as much as the body. It is not a mere ritual, but a means of drawing closer to Allah, where the barriers of the material world begin to dissolve.

Ibn Ata'illah, a prominent Sufi scholar, taught that prayer is a journey from distraction to presence, from heedlessness to divine awareness. He compared it to a candle in the darkness, illuminating the soul with divine light.

The Role of Khushu (Inner Presence)

One of the key mystical aspects of Salah is khushu—a state of deep humility and presence before Allah. The Qur'an states: "Successful indeed are the believers who are humble in their prayers" (23:1-2).

To attain khushu, the seeker must:

Focus the heart on Allah—Prayer should not be rushed but performed with mindfulness, as if one stands before the Divine Throne.

Internalize the meanings of recitations—Understanding the words deepens their impact, transforming the prayer from habit to devotion.

Practice sincerity (Ikhlas)—Prayer should be offered purely for Allah, not as a mere obligation.

The Mystical Symbolism of Movements in Salah

Each physical movement in prayer carries a spiritual meaning:

Takbir (raising hands to begin)—A symbolic surrender to Allah, letting go of worldly distractions.

Qiyam (standing)—A reminder of the Day of Judgment, where all stand before Allah.

Ruku (bowing)—A sign of humility, acknowledging one's dependence on the Creator.

Sujood (prostration)—The highest point of submission, where the self dissolves in the presence of Allah.

Tashahhud (final sitting)—A moment of spiritual witnessing, affirming the unity of Allah.

The Secret of Sujood

Among all the actions in Salah, prostration holds a unique place in mysticism. The Prophet (PBUH) said, "The closest a servant is to his Lord is while he is in prostration" (Muslim). Sufi teachings regard sujood as an annihilation of the ego (fana), where the worshipper symbolically dies to the world and awakens in divine proximity.

The Connection Between Salah and Light

Salah is often associated with divine light (nur). The Qur'an refers to it as a means of illuminating the heart: "Establish prayer for My remembrance" (20:14). Sufi scholars describe the prayers as waves of divine light washing over the soul, refining it with each cycle.

In mystical traditions, those who perform their prayers with devotion and sincerity begin to manifest an inner luminosity, visible not to the physical eye but perceived by the spiritually attuned.

The Impact of Salah on the Soul

When approached with spiritual awareness, prayer:

Purifies the heart—Cleansing it from heedlessness and attachments.

Strengthens divine connection—Bringing a constant awareness of Allah throughout the day.

Elevates the soul—Raising the believer from a state of distraction to divine presence.

Salah is not merely a duty; it is a divine invitation, a means of transformation, and a path toward intimacy with the Creator.

Chapter 17: The Influence of Imam Al-Ghazali on Sunni Mysticism

The Revival of Islamic Spirituality

Imam Abu Hamid Al-Ghazali (1058–1111) is one of the most influential scholars in the history of Sunni mysticism. His works bridged the gap between Islamic law (Shariah) and spirituality (Tazkiyah), offering a comprehensive path that emphasized both outward observance and inner purification.

Before Al-Ghazali, there was a growing rift between scholars of jurisprudence and the Sufis, with each group questioning the legitimacy of the other. His writings helped reconcile these perspectives, showing that true devotion to Allah required a balance of knowledge, practice, and inner transformation.

Al-Ghazali's Personal Journey

Despite achieving great success as a scholar, Al-Ghazali experienced a spiritual crisis that led him to abandon his prestigious position in Baghdad and embark on a period of seclusion and reflection. This phase of self-examination deeply influenced his later works, particularly Ihya' Ulum al-Din (The Revival of the Religious Sciences), which became a cornerstone of Sunni mysticism.

Key Teachings in Sunni Mysticism

Al-Ghazali's approach to Sufism was rooted in the Qur'an and Sunnah, emphasizing:

The Purification of the Heart – True knowledge is not just intellectual but must be accompanied by an inward transformation that cleanses the heart from spiritual diseases like arrogance, greed, and heedlessness.

Sincerity in Worship – Ritual acts must be performed with devotion and presence, rather than mere outward compliance.

The Concept of Ma'rifah (Divine Knowledge) – A higher state of consciousness that allows the seeker to perceive deeper truths about existence and the self.

Balancing Fear and Hope – A believer should fear Allah's justice but also remain hopeful in His mercy.

The Impact of Ihya' Ulum al-Din

The Revival of the Religious Sciences remains one of the most widely studied books in Islamic spirituality. It covers:

Acts of worship and their spiritual dimensions.

Ethical conduct and the refinement of character.

The dangers of worldly attachments and how to overcome them.

The path to attaining closeness to Allah through sincerity and discipline.

This work was pivotal in bringing mysticism back into the mainstream of Sunni thought, demonstrating that Sufi practices, when grounded in Islamic teachings, lead to a deeper, more meaningful faith.

Al-Ghazali's Lasting Legacy

His synthesis of knowledge and spirituality continues to inspire seekers of truth. He showed that true Sufism is not about abandoning religious obligations but about fulfilling them with deeper awareness. Through his writings, Al-Ghazali revived the essence of Islamic spirituality, leaving a legacy that endures across centuries.

Chapter 18: Understanding Barakah (Spiritual Blessings)

The Concept of Barakah in Islam

Barakah is a divine gift, an unseen spiritual presence that brings goodness, increase, and continuity in one's life. Rooted in the Qur'an and Sunnah, it is a manifestation of Allah's blessings that extends beyond material wealth to touch all aspects of existence. The Prophet Muhammad (PBUH) frequently prayed for barakah, teaching his followers that it is not merely about abundance, but about the quality and benefit derived from what one possesses.

Sources of Barakah

In Sunni mysticism, barakah is believed to emanate from several key sources:

Allah's Divine Will – Barakah is ultimately granted by Allah to whomever He wills.

The Qur'an and Sunnah – Engaging with divine revelation, whether through recitation, contemplation, or application, attracts blessings into one's life.

Righteous Actions – Acts of devotion such as prayer, charity, and honesty cultivate barakah in daily affairs.

The Presence of the Pious – Being in the company of righteous people, especially scholars and mystics, is said to bring spiritual blessings.

Time and Effort Spent in Worship – Seeking Allah in the early hours of the morning (tahajjud), maintaining sincerity in work, and dedicating oneself to service invite divine favor.

Barakah in Daily Life

The presence of barakah is not always visible but can be perceived through its effects. A meal shared in gratitude may sustain many, time devoted to seeking knowledge may yield deep wisdom, and wealth spent in charity may bring spiritual contentment beyond its numerical value.

Sunni mystics emphasize that true barakah is felt in the heart—it is the sense of fulfillment, peace, and divine nearness that accompanies a blessed life.

The Role of Barakah in Spiritual Growth

Barakah is not just a worldly blessing; it is also an aid in the spiritual journey. Those who live with sincerity and devotion often find their time, resources, and efforts miraculously expanded, allowing them to progress in their pursuit of divine proximity. Mystics teach that barakah strengthens patience, deepens faith, and illuminates the path of those who walk in remembrance of Allah.

By seeking barakah in all aspects of life—through sincerity, righteous deeds, and connection to the divine—one aligns with the greater flow of divine blessings, fostering a life of peace, contentment, and spiritual elevation.

Chapter 19: The Ethics of a Mystic: Simplicity, Generosity, and Patience

Simplicity as a Spiritual Principle

Simplicity is a core value in Sunni mysticism, reflecting detachment from material excess and a focus on the heart's purity. The Prophet Muhammad (PBUH) exemplified this virtue by living modestly despite his influence and status. Mystics believe that reducing worldly distractions allows the soul to focus on divine remembrance.

Sunni mystics practice simplicity not as an ascetic rejection of the world but as a means to avoid excessiveness and maintain sincerity in worship. They emphasize that a heart unburdened by greed and attachment to luxury finds it easier to cultivate spiritual awareness.

Generosity: Giving Without Expectation

Generosity in Sunni mysticism extends beyond material charity—it includes kindness, forgiveness, and the sharing of knowledge. The Qur'an frequently reminds believers that giving benefits the giver as much as the receiver.

The Prophet Muhammad (PBUH) stated, "The best of people are those who are most beneficial to others." Mystics internalize this teaching, seeing generosity as a reflection of divine mercy. They believe that giving freely, without seeking recognition, purifies the soul and strengthens one's connection to Allah.

Mystics practice generosity in various ways:

Material Giving – Supporting the needy and engaging in acts of charity (sadaqah and zakat).

Spiritual Guidance – Teaching and mentoring seekers without expecting compensation.

Time and Presence – Offering one's time to listen, console, and uplift others.

Patience: Endurance on the Path

Patience (sabr) is one of the most emphasized virtues in the Qur'an and a fundamental trait of those walking the mystical path. Mystics understand that spiritual growth is a gradual process, requiring perseverance through challenges.

Three dimensions of patience are particularly relevant in Sunni mysticism:

Patience in Worship – Consistency in prayer, dhikr, and devotion despite hardships.

Patience in Adversity – Enduring trials with trust in Allah's wisdom.

Patience with Others – Responding to harm or injustice with restraint and forgiveness.

Mystics believe that patience deepens faith, strengthens reliance on Allah, and purifies the heart. It transforms suffering into an opportunity for spiritual elevation and closeness to the Divine.

By cultivating simplicity, generosity, and patience, a mystic aligns their life with the values of the Prophet Muhammad (PBUH) and paves the way for a heart that is open, humble, and attuned to divine presence.

Chapter 20: The Interplay of Shariah and Haqiqah (Legal and Mystical Truth)

Understanding Shariah and Haqiqah

In Sunni mysticism, the relationship between Shariah (Islamic law) and Haqiqah (spiritual truth) is not one of opposition, but of harmony. Shariah provides the external framework for living a righteous life, while Haqiqah represents the inner realization of divine reality. Sunni mystics emphasize that true spiritual enlightenment does not abandon the legal foundations of Islam but rather deepens their understanding and application.

Shariah: The Path of Discipline

Shariah is the structured legal system derived from the Qur'an and Sunnah, governing all aspects of life, including worship, transactions, ethics, and personal conduct. It ensures that a believer maintains righteousness and accountability before Allah. Mystics see Shariah as the outer shell that protects and nurtures the soul, allowing it to grow spiritually while remaining grounded in divine commandments.

Practicing Shariah includes:

Performing the five daily prayers with sincerity and focus.

Observing halal and haram distinctions in daily life.

Upholding justice, honesty, and ethical behavior in all dealings.

Engaging in acts of worship as a means of drawing closer to Allah.

Haqiqah: The Inner Reality

Haqiqah refers to the deeper, spiritual truths that a believer seeks to uncover through devotion and inner purification. It is the understanding of Allah's presence in all aspects of existence and the realization of one's complete dependence on Him. Haqiqah is cultivated through remembrance (dhikr), reflection, and love of the Divine.

Mystics view Haqiqah as:

The knowledge that all existence is a manifestation of Allah's will.

The purification of the heart from ego and worldly attachments.
The experience of divine love and closeness to Allah.
The unveiling of deeper meanings within the Qur'an and Hadith.

The Balance Between the Outward and Inward

Sunni mystics caution against neglecting Shariah in the pursuit of Haqiqah. They believe that without the discipline of Shariah, one risks falling into spiritual delusions, whereas without Haqiqah, one's religious practice may become mechanical and devoid of inner meaning. A true seeker integrates both, ensuring that their external obedience aligns with their internal awakening.

The great mystic Imam Al-Ghazali described this balance as essential for attaining true piety, teaching that the law (fiqh) and inner wisdom (ma'rifah) must complement one another. Sunni Sufis emphasize that the mystical path is not a rejection of Islamic law but an elevation of its deeper purpose—bringing the believer closer to Allah in both action and heart.

By embracing both Shariah and Haqiqah, a believer walks a path that is both disciplined and illuminated, ensuring that legal observance is infused with spiritual depth and that mystical experiences remain rooted in divine guidance.

Chapter 21: Sufi Poetry and Its Spiritual Impact

Poetry as a Medium for Spiritual Expression

Poetry has been a powerful tool for conveying the essence of Sunni mysticism. It transcends mere words, acting as a vessel for divine wisdom and love. Sufi poets have used poetry to express their yearning for Allah, their struggles on the spiritual path, and their realizations of divine presence.

Mystics believe that poetry engages the heart in a way that logical discourse sometimes cannot. It moves beyond intellectual understanding, reaching into the depths of the soul. This is why many Sufi teachers have employed poetry to inspire their disciples and awaken them to spiritual truths.

Notable Sunni Sufi Poets

Several great poets have shaped the landscape of Sufi poetry, leaving behind works that continue to guide seekers on their path to Allah. Among them:

Jalal al-Din Rumi – Although often associated with Persian mysticism, Rumi's poetry embodies Sunni teachings, emphasizing love as the path to divine union. His verses encourage surrender to Allah's will.

Shaykh Sa'di – A master of wisdom literature, Sa'di's poetry blends ethical teachings with mystical insight, teaching that true spirituality must be reflected in everyday conduct.

Imam Al-Busiri – His Qasidah al-Burda remains one of the most revered Arabic poems in Islamic history, expressing deep love for the Prophet Muhammad (PBUH).

Allama Iqbal – His works revive the essence of spiritual awakening, encouraging self-realization and devotion to Allah.

Themes in Sufi Poetry

Sufi poetry explores many profound themes, including:

Divine Love – The relationship between the soul and Allah is often likened to a lover seeking the Beloved. This intense longing is seen as the heart's deepest desire.

Separation and Union – Many poems express the pain of separation from the Divine and the ecstasy of reuniting with Him.

The Spiritual Journey – Poetry often describes the struggles, obstacles, and victories of the seeker in their quest for closeness to Allah.

The Illusion of the World – Poets warn against attachment to the material world, emphasizing its transient nature compared to the eternal reality of Allah.

The Role of Poetry in Sufi Practice

In Sunni mysticism, poetry is not merely for artistic appreciation—it serves as a means of spiritual reflection. Many Sufi gatherings incorporate poetry as part of their dhikr, using rhythmic verses to focus the mind and heart on Allah. The repetition of certain lines in poetry can lead to deep contemplation, unlocking hidden layers of meaning within the words.

Sufi poetry remains a timeless guide, offering wisdom and inspiration for those seeking to understand the mysteries of the Divine.

Chapter 22: The Role of Music and Qawwali in Sunni Mysticism

The Place of Music in Sunni Mysticism

In Sunni mysticism, music is regarded as a means to elevate the soul and draw closer to Allah. While strict interpretations of Islamic law caution against excessive indulgence in music, many Sunni Sufi traditions have incorporated it as a powerful tool for spiritual awakening. When used with the right intention, music serves as a vehicle for contemplation, devotion, and divine love.

Sufis believe that music, when aligned with the remembrance of Allah, can stir the heart and lead to a state of heightened spiritual awareness. It is not the melody itself that holds value, but the ability of sound and rhythm to awaken inner emotions and direct them toward divine truths.

The Tradition of Qawwali

Qawwali is one of the most recognized forms of Sufi devotional music, originating in South Asia. It is a form of musical expression that blends poetry, rhythm, and repetition to create an immersive experience. Qawwali performances often take place in Sufi shrines and gatherings, aiming to inspire love for Allah and His Messenger.

Key elements of Qawwali include:

Praise of Allah and the Prophet (PBUH) – The lyrics often glorify Allah and recount the virtues of the Prophet Muhammad (PBUH).

Metaphors for Divine Love – Many songs use symbolic language, where earthly love represents the soul's yearning for the Divine.

Call and Response – The interaction between the lead singer and the chorus mirrors the communal nature of mystical gatherings.

Repetition for Spiritual Impact – Certain phrases or verses are repeated to reinforce their meaning and induce a trance-like state.

The Spiritual Effect of Sufi Music

The impact of music in Sufi practice extends beyond entertainment; it is a means of achieving wajd (spiritual ecstasy). In moments of deep emotional connection, listeners may experience an overwhelming sense of divine presence, sometimes leading to physical expressions such as swaying, tears, or exclamations of devotion.

Sufi saints and scholars have discussed the power of sound in influencing the heart. Imam Al-Ghazali, for instance, acknowledged that music, when used correctly, can awaken love for Allah and soften the heart. However, he also warned that it should not lead to heedlessness or indulgence in worldly desires.

Balancing Music with Islamic Teachings

While some scholars have debated the permissibility of music, Sunni mystics emphasize the importance of intention. If music serves to remind one of Allah, deepen spiritual awareness, and encourage righteous action, it is seen as a beneficial practice. Conversely, if it distracts from worship or leads to sinful behavior, it should be avoided.

Ultimately, the use of music in Sunni mysticism is a reflection of its broader philosophy—uniting the outer practice of Shariah with the inner experience of Haqiqah. It serves as a bridge between the material and the spiritual, helping seekers find divine connection through the rhythm of the heart.

Chapter 23: The Concept of Nur (Divine Light)

The Meaning of Nur in Islamic Mysticism

Nur, meaning "light" in Arabic, holds profound spiritual significance in Sunni mysticism. It symbolizes divine presence, guidance, and truth, illuminating the hearts of believers who seek closeness to Allah. The Quran frequently mentions light as a metaphor for divine knowledge and guidance, most notably in the Ayat al-Nur (24:35), where Allah describes Himself as the Light of the heavens and the earth.

Sufi scholars interpret this verse as a reflection of how divine illumination reaches the hearts of the spiritually aware, leading them from ignorance to enlightenment. This light is not physical but a metaphysical reality that cleanses the soul and unveils hidden truths.

Nur as a Spiritual Reality

In Sunni mysticism, Nur is understood as both an internal and external phenomenon. Internally, it manifests as an increased awareness of Allah's presence, clarity of heart, and purity of intention. Externally, it can be seen in the wisdom and serenity of those who have attained high spiritual ranks. Many Sufis believe that the faces of the righteous radiate with this light due to their devotion and sincerity in worship.

The Prophet Muhammad (PBUH) is often described as the pinnacle of divine light, as his presence brought spiritual awakening to humanity. Sunni mystics emphasize that his actions, character, and teachings continue to serve as a source of guidance, illuminating the path for believers.

Attaining Nur Through Spiritual Practices

The journey to acquiring divine light requires effort and sincerity. Sunni mystics teach that this illumination is granted to those who dedicate themselves to spiritual refinement. Key practices that cultivate Nur include:

Sincere Worship – Acts of worship such as prayer, fasting, and dhikr cleanse the heart and allow divine light to penetrate the soul.

Seeking Knowledge – Gaining knowledge of the Quran, Hadith, and spiritual teachings enhances one's awareness of divine truths.

Purification of the Heart – Removing arrogance, envy, and other negative traits makes the heart a vessel for receiving divine light.

Service to Others – Helping those in need and embodying the ethics of Islam allow the light of Allah to manifest in one's actions.

Signs of a Heart Illuminated by Nur

A heart blessed with Nur exhibits distinct characteristics:

Clarity in Understanding – The ability to distinguish between truth and falsehood with ease.

Serenity and Contentment – A deep sense of inner peace despite external challenges.

Attraction to Righteousness – A natural inclination towards good deeds and avoiding sin.

Radiance in Conduct – A luminous presence that brings comfort to others.

Sunni mysticism teaches that divine light is not limited to the chosen few but is accessible to all who sincerely seek Allah's guidance. By striving for purity in thought, action, and devotion, the seeker can walk the path illuminated by Nur.

Chapter 24: Dreams and Visions in Sufi Spirituality

The Role of Dreams in Islamic Mysticism

Dreams have always been considered a powerful medium of divine communication in Islamic spirituality. The Prophet Muhammad (PBUH) emphasized their significance, stating that true dreams are a form of prophecy. In Sunni mysticism, dreams provide guidance, warnings, and insights into the unseen world, offering the seeker a glimpse of deeper spiritual realities.

Visions as Signs of Spiritual Awakening

Sufi mystics describe visions (mukashafat) as moments when the veils of the material world are lifted, allowing them to perceive divine truths. These experiences are not sought for their own sake but arise naturally through intense devotion and purification of the heart. Many prominent Sufis have recorded visionary encounters with the Prophet Muhammad (PBUH), righteous saints, or symbolic representations of spiritual states.

Interpretation of Dreams in Sufi Tradition

Sunni mystics follow specific guidelines when interpreting dreams:

Symbolism Over Literal Meaning – Dreams often communicate through metaphors rather than direct messages.

Alignment with Shariah – True spiritual dreams never contradict Islamic teachings.

State of the Dreamer – The purity of one's heart influences the clarity and truthfulness of dreams.

Guidance from Scholars – Dream interpretation is best understood with the insight of knowledgeable scholars or spiritual mentors.

The Connection Between the Heart and Dreams

Sufi teachings emphasize that a heart free from worldly distractions is more likely to receive truthful dreams. Practices such as dhikr, prayer, and self-discipline refine the soul, making it a clearer receptacle for divine messages. Those who maintain a high state of spiritual consciousness often report profound and life-changing dreams.

Through dreams and visions, Sunni mysticism highlights the connection between the seen and unseen worlds, affirming the ever-present guidance of Allah in the life of the seeker.

Chapter 25: The Science of the Heart (Ilm al-Qalb)

The Heart as the Center of Spiritual Awareness

In Sunni mysticism, the heart (qalb) is considered the seat of spiritual knowledge and awareness. Unlike the physical heart, the qalb refers to the inner essence of a person, the place where divine wisdom resides. The Quran frequently references the heart in relation to faith, guidance, and inner purification, highlighting its central role in a believer's journey toward Allah.

Sunni mystics emphasize that the qalb is not merely an organ but a vessel capable of receiving divine light and understanding. It is through the heart that one experiences deep spiritual truths and draws closer to Allah. However, this requires purification, as the heart can be clouded by sin, distractions, and attachment to the material world.

The Three States of the Heart

Islamic scholars and Sufi masters categorize the heart into three primary states, each representing different levels of spiritual refinement:

Qalb al-Salim (The Sound Heart): This is a heart free from corruption, filled with sincerity and devotion to Allah. A person with a qalb al-salim is in constant remembrance of Allah and possesses a deep sense of peace.

Qalb al-Mayyit (The Dead Heart): This heart is devoid of spiritual life, disconnected from divine guidance. It is filled with heedlessness, arrogance, and desires that distance it from Allah's mercy.

Qalb al-Marid (The Diseased Heart): This heart is in a state of struggle, fluctuating between faith and worldly distractions. It requires healing through remembrance of Allah, repentance, and spiritual discipline.

The Process of Heart Purification

Sunni mysticism teaches that purifying the heart is a gradual process requiring sincere effort and divine assistance. Some of the key methods for cleansing the heart include:

Dhikr (Remembrance of Allah): Regular recitation of Allah's names and Quranic verses refines the heart and increases spiritual awareness.

Tawbah (Repentance): Seeking forgiveness from Allah for past sins removes spiritual stains from the heart.

Suhbah (Spiritual Companionship): Surrounding oneself with righteous individuals helps maintain a pure and sincere heart.

Muraqaba (Spiritual Reflection): Engaging in introspection and self-accountability strengthens the connection between the heart and Allah.

The Role of the Heart in Divine Knowledge

The qalb is considered the primary vessel for divine knowledge (ma'rifah). While intellectual understanding is valuable, true comprehension of spiritual realities comes through an enlightened heart. Sunni mystics emphasize that knowledge gained through the heart leads to deeper faith, certainty (yaqin), and love for Allah.

A purified heart allows the seeker to perceive divine wisdom in everyday experiences, recognizing signs of Allah's presence in creation. This level of awareness transforms one's character, fostering humility, patience, and a profound sense of gratitude.

The science of the heart in Sunni mysticism is ultimately a path of self-purification and divine proximity. Those who embark on this journey seek to align their inner being with the will of Allah, striving for a heart that reflects His light and guidance.

Chapter 26: The Power of Istighfar (Seeking Forgiveness)

The Meaning and Importance of Istighfar

Istighfar, the act of seeking forgiveness from Allah, is a central practice in Sunni mysticism. It is not merely a verbal expression but a profound state of repentance that purifies the soul and brings a person closer to Allah. The Quran repeatedly encourages believers to engage in istighfar, as it is a means of attaining divine mercy and spiritual elevation.

Mystics emphasize that seeking forgiveness is not only for those who have sinned but also for those who wish to elevate their spiritual states. Even the Prophet Muhammad (PBUH), who was free of sin, regularly sought forgiveness, teaching his followers the importance of humility and dependence on Allah's mercy.

Istighfar as a Form of Spiritual Cleansing

Sunni mysticism views istighfar as a method of purifying the heart and soul. Just as dirt accumulates on the body, sins and heedlessness accumulate on the heart, creating barriers between a person and divine enlightenment. Frequent istighfar removes these barriers, allowing the seeker to maintain a clear spiritual connection with Allah.

The practice of istighfar can take many forms, including:

Reciting phrases such as Astaghfirullah (I seek forgiveness from Allah).

Offering sincere repentance with the intention of not repeating past mistakes.

Seeking forgiveness for the community and humanity as a whole, recognizing the interconnectedness of all souls.

The Transformative Effects of Istighfar

Engaging in regular istighfar has numerous spiritual and worldly benefits. Some of these include:

Inner Peace: Removing guilt and remorse allows the seeker to experience tranquility.

Increased Provision: The Quran mentions that those who seek forgiveness will find their sustenance increased.

Strengthened Relationship with Allah: A repentant heart is more receptive to divine guidance.

Mystics believe that true istighfar transforms the seeker, making them more conscious of their actions and more compassionate toward others. By constantly seeking Allah's forgiveness, the mystic aligns their soul with divine mercy, striving toward spiritual perfection.

Chapter 27: The Relationship Between Mysticism and Society

Balancing Spirituality and Social Responsibility

Sunni mysticism does not advocate complete withdrawal from society but rather emphasizes a balance between inner purification and active engagement with the world. Many prominent Sunni mystics, including figures like Abdul Qadir Jilani and Rumi, were deeply involved in their communities, guiding people spiritually while also addressing social and ethical concerns.

A mystic is not only a seeker of personal enlightenment but also a servant to humanity. Engaging in acts of kindness, social justice, and community service is viewed as an extension of one's devotion to Allah. This balance ensures that spirituality does not become an isolated endeavor but a force for positive transformation.

The Role of Mystics in Social Reform

Throughout Islamic history, Sufi scholars and saints have played key roles in addressing injustice, oppression, and moral corruption. Many established institutions such as schools, hospitals, and shelters, recognizing that faith is not just about personal piety but also about uplifting society.

Mystics have often acted as mediators during conflicts, using their spiritual authority to promote peace and reconciliation. Their teachings emphasize humility, justice, and service, inspiring rulers and common people alike to uphold ethical values.

The Concept of 'Serving Creation'

One of the core principles of Sunni mysticism is that serving creation is an act of devotion to the Creator. The famous saying, "The best among you are those who are most beneficial to others," reflects this mystical ideal. Providing for the needy, helping the sick, and offering counsel are all seen as spiritual acts that purify the soul.

Mystics believe that spiritual enlightenment should not lead to arrogance or detachment from worldly concerns but should manifest in selfless service. This philosophy has been reflected in countless Sufi orders, where charity and hospitality are foundational practices.

The Influence of Mysticism on Culture and Ethics

Sunni mysticism has left a profound mark on art, literature, and moral philosophy. The teachings of Sufi poets like Rumi, Saadi, and Hafiz continue to inspire ethical reflection and spiritual growth. Their works promote universal values of love, tolerance, and compassion, influencing not only Islamic societies but also cultures across the world.

Ethically, mysticism fosters patience, humility, and gratitude. It discourages materialism and selfishness, advocating instead for a life of simplicity and generosity. Many Sufi traditions emphasize that true wealth lies not in possessions but in a heart enriched by divine love and service to others.

The Contemporary Relevance of Mysticism in Society

In the modern era, Sunni mysticism offers a spiritual antidote to the anxieties and materialistic excesses of contemporary life. As people seek deeper meaning beyond economic success and social status, the teachings of mysticism provide guidance on inner peace, mindfulness, and ethical living.

Mystical communities continue to engage in humanitarian efforts, interfaith dialogue, and social justice work, demonstrating that the wisdom of the past remains highly relevant today. By bridging spirituality with action, Sunni mysticism ensures that faith remains a guiding force for both personal and societal well-being.

Chapter 28: Women in Sunni Mysticism

The Role of Women in Early Islamic Mysticism

Women have played a crucial role in the development of Sunni mysticism, serving as scholars, spiritual guides, and exemplars of piety. One of the earliest and most revered figures is Rabi'a al-Adawiyya (d. 801), whose deep devotion and teachings on divine love continue to influence Sufi thought. She rejected material wealth and emphasized complete reliance on Allah, inspiring generations of seekers.

Historically, women have participated in Sufi circles, often holding positions of leadership in spiritual gatherings. They have contributed to Islamic scholarship, written poetry, and taught disciples, demonstrating that mysticism transcends gender barriers.

Female Mystics and Their Contributions

Beyond Rabi'a al-Adawiyya, many women have made significant contributions to Sunni mysticism. Sayyida Nafisa (d. 824), a renowned scholar and spiritual teacher in Egypt, was highly respected by both Sufi and non-Sufi scholars. Fatima al-Nisaburi was another influential figure, known for her wisdom and ability to guide others on the spiritual path.

Women have composed mystical poetry, engaged in social welfare, and established Sufi lodges (khaniqahs) where both men and women sought spiritual education. In various Sufi orders, women have served as mentors, passing down knowledge and spiritual practices to the next generations.

Women in Sufi Orders

Although some Sufi orders have been male-dominated, many have included women in both formal and informal capacities. The Chishti and Qadiri orders, in particular, have historically allowed women to participate in gatherings of remembrance (dhikr) and spiritual instruction. Some Sufi orders, such as the Shadhiliyyah, have recorded instances of women attaining high levels of spiritual realization.

Women have often been recognized as saints, their tombs becoming places of pilgrimage where devotees seek blessings (barakah). Their legacies live on in oral traditions, poetry, and hagiographies that recount their piety, wisdom, and closeness to Allah.

The Ethical and Mystical Teachings of Female Saints

The teachings of female Sunni mystics emphasize themes of divine love, humility, and service to others. Many female saints have stressed the importance of sincerity (ikhlas) and detachment from worldly distractions. Their insights align with the broader principles of Sunni mysticism, which advocates purification of the heart and selfless devotion to Allah.

Women mystics have also contributed to ethical discourse, advocating for justice, compassion, and social harmony. Their wisdom has influenced not only their immediate disciples but also wider Islamic intellectual traditions.

Women in Contemporary Sunni Mysticism

In modern times, women continue to play a vital role in Sunni mysticism. Female scholars and spiritual teachers conduct gatherings, publish works on Islamic spirituality, and engage in interfaith dialogue. Women's participation in Sufi practices has expanded globally, with many seeking spiritual fulfillment through traditional paths of Sunni mysticism.

Despite challenges, contemporary female mystics uphold the rich legacy of their predecessors, demonstrating that the pursuit of divine love and knowledge is not limited by gender. They continue to inspire, educate, and guide seekers on the path of spiritual realization.

Chapter 29: Sunni Mysticism and Interfaith Dialogue

The Foundation of Interfaith Engagement in Sunni Mysticism

Sunni mysticism has historically emphasized the unity of humanity and the universality of divine truth. This perspective has led many Sunni Sufis to engage in interfaith dialogue, recognizing shared ethical and spiritual values among different religious traditions. The Qur'an itself acknowledges diversity as part of Allah's plan: "To each among you, We have prescribed a law and a clear way. If Allah had willed, He would have made you one nation" (5:48). This verse has often been interpreted by Sunni mystics as a call to respect and engage with other faiths.

Historical Examples of Interfaith Interaction

Throughout Islamic history, Sufi scholars and saints have engaged in dialogue with followers of other religious traditions. Figures like Jalal al-Din Rumi (d. 1273) and Ibn Arabi (d. 1240) wrote extensively about divine love in ways that resonated with Christians, Jews, Hindus, and other spiritual traditions. In South Asia, the Chishti Sufi order became known for fostering harmonious relations with Hindu communities, promoting an inclusive spiritual ethos.

In the Ottoman Empire, Sufi orders such as the Mevlevi (followers of Rumi) were active in diplomatic and intellectual exchanges with Christian and Jewish scholars. Their teachings emphasized inner transformation and the oneness of God, which created common ground for interfaith discourse.

Principles of Mystical Interfaith Engagement

Sunni mysticism approaches interfaith dialogue with a few core principles:

Recognition of the Divine in All Beings: Many Sufis believe that divine love manifests in all creation, making it essential to respect people of all backgrounds.

Dialogue Through the Heart: Rather than focusing on theological debates, Sufis prioritize shared experiences of love, devotion, and remembrance of God.

Ethical and Social Cooperation: Sunni mystics have often worked alongside other faith groups in charity, education, and peacemaking efforts.

Contemporary Sunni Mysticism and Interfaith Work

Today, Sunni mystics continue to be involved in interfaith initiatives worldwide. Sufi leaders participate in international forums on religious harmony, while Sufi music, poetry, and literature are used as bridges between cultures. Their approach reflects a commitment to spiritual inclusivity while remaining rooted in the principles of Islamic faith.

Chapter 30: Common Misconceptions About Sufism

Sufism as a Separate Sect

One of the most prevalent misconceptions is that Sufism constitutes a separate sect within Islam. In reality, Sunni Sufism is deeply rooted in Islamic teachings and aligns with the Qur'an and Sunnah. Sufism is not a different branch of Islam but rather an approach to deepening one's spirituality within the Sunni framework. Many well-known scholars, such as Imam Al-Ghazali and Shah Waliullah, integrated Sufism with mainstream Islamic scholarship.

Sufism and Innovation (Bid'ah)

Some critics claim that Sufism introduces religious innovations (bid'ah) that deviate from Islamic teachings. However, traditional Sunni Sufis adhere to Shariah while practicing spiritual purification and inner devotion. Authentic Sufi practices derive from the Qur'an, Hadith, and the example of the Prophet Muhammad (PBUH). While cultural influences may shape different Sufi expressions, the core principles remain rooted in Islamic tradition.

Worship of Saints

Another misconception is that Sufis worship saints or their tombs. In reality, Sunni Sufism does not promote saint worship; rather, visiting the graves of righteous individuals is seen as a means of seeking blessings (barakah) and inspiration. Sufis believe in tawheed (the oneness of God) and do not attribute divinity to any human being. The respect shown to saints is similar to the reverence given to scholars and righteous figures in Islamic history.

Sufism as Passive or Detached from Society

Some view Sufism as an entirely passive practice, disconnected from social responsibilities. While contemplation and seclusion (khalwah) are part of Sufi traditions, many Sunni Sufi figures have been active in their communities, promoting education, justice, and social reform. Sufi scholars have historically played roles in governance, charity work, and peacemaking efforts, demonstrating that spirituality and societal engagement go hand in hand.

The Role of Music and Poetry

There is a misconception that Sufism universally promotes music and dancing as acts of worship. While some Sufi traditions use music and poetry as tools for spiritual elevation, other Sunni Sufi orders emphasize silent remembrance (dhikr) and contemplation. The acceptance or rejection of music varies within Islamic jurisprudence, and Sufism itself does not mandate any specific form of artistic expression.

Sufism and Mystical Experiences

Some believe that Sufism is solely about supernatural experiences or miracles (karamat). While some Sufi saints are known for extraordinary events, the true essence of Sunni Sufism lies in ethical conduct, self-discipline, and devotion to Allah. The goal is not to seek mystical phenomena but to attain closeness to Allah through sincerity, patience, and worship.

Sunni Sufism and Extremism

Another modern misconception is that Sufism is either overly mystical or completely opposed to more traditional Islamic teachings. In reality, Sunni Sufism balances inner spirituality with outward adherence to the Sunnah. Throughout history, Sufi scholars have defended orthodox Islamic beliefs while emphasizing inner purification. Sufism, at its core, opposes extremism and promotes love, tolerance, and moderation.

The Universal Appeal of Sunni Sufism

Despite misconceptions, Sunni Sufism has remained an essential part of Islamic spirituality. It continues to inspire individuals across different cultures and backgrounds, providing a path to inner peace, devotion, and ethical living. By understanding the true nature of Sufism, seekers can appreciate its role in strengthening faith and enhancing the practice of Islam.

Chapter 31: Challenges and Criticism of Sunni Mysticism

The Perceived Conflict Between Sufism and Islamic Law

One of the primary challenges facing Sunni mysticism is the perception that it conflicts with Islamic law (Shariah). Some critics argue that Sufis emphasize personal experience over legalistic adherence. However, classical Sunni Sufis like Imam Al-Ghazali and Sheikh Abdul Qadir Jilani have demonstrated that true mysticism complements, rather than contradicts, Islamic law. While some fringe groups have strayed from orthodoxy, mainstream Sunni Sufism remains grounded in the Qur'an and Sunnah.

Modern Secularism and the Decline of Spirituality

With the rise of secular ideologies, spiritual practices such as dhikr (remembrance of God) and muraqabah (meditation) are often dismissed as outdated. The materialist worldview prioritizes tangible success over inner purification, leading many to view Sufism as impractical. Despite this, Sufi teachings continue to provide solace and meaning to those seeking spiritual depth in an increasingly fast-paced world.

Misuse and Commercialization of Sufi Practices

In some parts of the world, Sufism has been commercialized or misrepresented for political or financial gain. Some individuals exploit Sufi teachings to establish cult-like followings, deviating from the essence of humility and sincerity that define true mysticism. Additionally, the commercialization of Sufi music and poetry has sometimes stripped them of their deeper spiritual significance, reducing them to mere entertainment.

The Challenge of Extremist Rejection

Certain extremist movements reject Sufism outright, viewing it as a deviation from Islam. This has led to ideological attacks and even physical violence against Sufi shrines and gatherings in some regions.

Extremists oppose the emphasis on love, tolerance, and interfaith dialogue that characterize Sunni Sufism, creating an environment where Sufis must navigate hostility while upholding their traditions.

Internal Divisions and Sectarian Misunderstandings

Within Sunni mysticism, there exist different Sufi orders (tariqas), each with its unique approach to spiritual discipline. While these variations enrich the tradition, they sometimes lead to misunderstandings or rivalries. Instead of focusing on shared principles, certain groups become overly attached to specific teachers or practices, leading to unnecessary divisions.

The Influence of Western Rationalism

The rise of rationalist and scientific thought has led some to question the metaphysical aspects of Sufism, such as spiritual visions, karamat (miracles), and divine inspiration. Critics argue that these elements lack empirical evidence, dismissing them as superstition. While Sufism is not opposed to reason, it maintains that spiritual realities cannot always be measured through material means alone.

Balancing Mysticism and Practical Life

Some believe that embracing Sufism requires complete withdrawal from worldly affairs. However, the challenge for many Sufis today is finding balance—engaging in daily responsibilities while maintaining a deep connection with Allah. Classical Sunni Sufis emphasized that a true seeker does not abandon societal duties but rather integrates spirituality into every aspect of life.

The Future of Sunni Mysticism

Despite these challenges, Sunni mysticism continues to thrive, adapting to modern contexts while preserving its essence. By addressing misconceptions and reaffirming its connection to mainstream Islamic teachings, Sunni Sufism can remain a vital source of spiritual guidance for generations to come.

Chapter 32: Modern Sunni Mystics and Their Contributions

The Continuation of Sunni Mysticism in the Contemporary Era

Sunni mysticism is not a relic of the past; it continues to evolve and influence the modern world. In recent times, various scholars and spiritual guides have played a crucial role in preserving the essence of Sufism while addressing contemporary challenges. These individuals have sought to balance tradition with modernity, demonstrating that Sufi principles remain relevant in an ever-changing world.

Influential Sunni Mystics of the 20th and 21st Centuries

Several notable Sunni mystics and scholars have emerged in recent history, advocating for a deeper understanding of Tasawwuf while remaining firmly rooted in orthodox Islam. Figures such as Sheikh Ahmad al-Alawi of Algeria, Sheikh Muhammad Sa'id Ramadan al-Bouti of Syria, and Sheikh Nuh Ha Mim Keller have worked to bring Sufi teachings to contemporary audiences. Their writings and guidance emphasize the necessity of purifying the heart while actively engaging in the world.

The Revival of Classical Sufi Teachings

Many modern Sunni mystics have sought to reintroduce the wisdom of classical scholars such as Imam Al-Ghazali, Sheikh Abdul Qadir Jilani, and Jalal al-Din Rumi. Through books, lectures, and online platforms, they have provided access to timeless spiritual knowledge, ensuring that new generations benefit from the insights of past masters. These efforts have played a significant role in countering misconceptions about Sufism and reaffirming its place within mainstream Sunni Islam.

The Role of Digital Media in Spreading Mystical Teachings

In the digital age, social media, podcasts, and online courses have become tools for spreading Sufi teachings. Many modern mystics and scholars use these platforms to discuss concepts like dhikr, tawakkul, and purification of the heart. The accessibility of these teachings has allowed people from diverse backgrounds to engage with Sunni mysticism, often leading them to pursue deeper study and practice.

Addressing Contemporary Spiritual Crises

The modern world presents unique spiritual challenges, including materialism, mental health struggles, and a sense of detachment from faith. Many Sunni mystics today address these concerns by offering guidance on how to integrate spirituality into daily life. By emphasizing the inner dimensions of worship and the transformative power of divine remembrance, they provide solutions that resonate with contemporary seekers.

Interfaith and Cross-Cultural Contributions

Modern Sunni mystics have also played a role in interfaith dialogue and cross-cultural exchanges. Figures such as Sheikh Hamza Yusuf and Sheikh Abdal Hakim Murad have contributed to discussions on spirituality, ethics, and global harmony, demonstrating how Sufi principles align with universal values of compassion and wisdom. Their work has helped bridge gaps between different faith traditions while reinforcing the depth of Islamic spirituality.

The Future of Sunni Mysticism

As the world continues to change, the role of Sunni mystics remains vital. Their ability to adapt traditional teachings to contemporary contexts ensures that the essence of Tasawwuf remains alive. Whether through literature, digital media, or personal mentorship, modern Sunni mystics continue to guide seekers on the path of spiritual refinement and divine love.

Chapter 33: Conclusion: Walking the Path of Light

The Timeless Relevance of Sunni Mysticism

Sunni mysticism remains a guiding force for those seeking a deeper connection with Allah. Through the practice of Tasawwuf, believers have found ways to refine their character, strengthen their faith, and draw closer to the Divine. The teachings of the past continue to illuminate the path for modern seekers, proving that the spiritual wisdom of Islam is timeless.

Integrating Mysticism into Daily Life

The principles of Tasawwuf are not meant to be confined to books or academic discussions—they are meant to be lived. Practicing gratitude, engaging in dhikr, and embodying the ethics of humility and compassion help bridge the gap between knowledge and experience. Sunni mysticism teaches that spirituality is not separate from daily life; rather, it infuses every action with purpose and sincerity.

The Role of Community and Brotherhood

One of the key strengths of Sunni mysticism is the emphasis on brotherhood and spiritual companionship. The presence of a Murshid and a community of seekers provides invaluable support, ensuring that individuals do not walk the spiritual path alone. This collective journey fosters accountability, love, and sincerity, reinforcing the belief that true growth is achieved through mutual encouragement.

Overcoming Modern Spiritual Challenges

In a world driven by materialism and distractions, the teachings of Sunni mysticism offer a refuge for the heart and soul. The pursuit of inner peace, divine love, and self-awareness counters the restlessness of contemporary life. Through the wisdom of past scholars and the guidance of present-day mystics, individuals can navigate the complexities of the modern era without losing sight of their ultimate purpose.

Continuing the Journey

The path of light in Sunni mysticism does not end with the study of its principles—it continues through action, sincerity, and devotion. By embodying the virtues of patience, gratitude, and remembrance, seekers move closer to the ultimate goal: nearness to Allah. The journey of Tasawwuf is lifelong, and every step taken with sincerity is a step toward divine fulfillment.